C903579263

D1639403

DISCARDED

AWAY & AWARE

AWAY & AWARE

A FIELD GUIDE TO MINDFUL TRAVEL

BY SARA CLEMENCE

ILLUSTRATIONS BY CHRIS SANTONE

piatkus

CONTENTS

INTRODUCTION

This book is not about the where.

It won't give you insight into destination resorts or zip-lining tours. There are many guidebooks, websites, and apps designed to help you with those kinds of decisions—in fact, way too many. And that's part of the problem.

We're living in an age of information inundation. Any question can be answered in an instant (with varying degrees of reliability). We can view and "like" a photograph taken on the other side of the world in the same amount of time it takes to press a camera shutter release. We can receive messages at any time of the day from anywhere in the world, or talk to our friends in every corner of the globe—video face to video face!—whenever we feel the urge. The blessing of technology is that we can be connected all the time; its curse is that now we're expected to be.

On average, Americans check their phones about 50 times a day (and if you're reading this book, you probably check yours even more frequently). And they don't stop when they're away from home. Not only does our work follow us on our travels, but our habits—checking the news, browsing YouTube videos, snapping selfies to post online—do too. Ask people why they travel and they probably won't say their goal is to skim the surface of a foreign culture and take photos to share on Facebook, all the while answering office emails. Yet too often that's the reality.

So, unlike almost every travel book, this one is not about where to go, but *how* to go. I call this approach "mindful travel," but you might also call it slow travel, authentic travel, or traveling with integrity. It's about being more connected with your surroundings than with your devices and social media feeds—about enjoying the moment rather than racing through a checklist of tourist sites.

The book is an antidote to the contemporary afflictions of narcissism and alienation. It's a guide to dedigitizing your journeys and rediscovering analog pleasures—like people, pencils, and old-fashioned maps. It applies to any destination and any budget and is organized like a journey itself, starting with the planning process and ending with the return home. You can read it all the way through, dip in and out as you consider different aspects of your trip, or peek at random pages. Whether you're planning a camping trip in the mountains or an eating excursion to Italy, you will find something relevant.

Travel should make your heart bigger and your mind broader. It's a way of connecting with yourself—of learning who you are when you're not surrounded by your friends, your things, and your job. Along the way you will likely discover not only a charming town or a wonderful restaurant but also something about your resources, your temperament, your courage, and your curiosity.

Being a mindful traveler isn't good just for you. It will make you a more considerate and respectful visitor, attentive to the people you meet and the places you see. You will be both consuming and sharing. It will, I hope, make you a traveler instead of a tourist.

CHAPTER ONE:
PLANNING YOUR ESCAPE

IDENTIFY YOUR INTENTION

It may sound like the start of a yoga class, but it's the most important part of the trip-planning process. And you should set aside mental space for it, just like you'd make time to figure out your flights.

Your intention is the purpose of your trip. It's less a single goal (I want to climb Mount Kilimanjaro) than an expression of overarching values (I want to push my physical limits). Along your journey, you'll be checking in with your intention to make sure what you're doing aligns with what you really want.

Keep your intention simple, and aim for clarity: I want to break unhealthy habits. I plan to immerse myself in a foreign culture. I hope to blow up my comfort zone.

Finally, write it down to make it official.

DO A DEEP DIVE

Explore as much of your destination as you can before you leave—and that doesn't mean digging through online hotel reviews. Read about the history and architecture of the place you'll be visiting, listen to the local music, research the local food scene, peruse news sites, and tune in to radio stations. Look for fiction by native authors. If you get familiar with the culture, politics, and cuisine, you'll feel (almost) like a local by the time you arrive.

VISIT UNCONNECTED DESTINATIONS

Want to get off the digital treadmill? You don't have to rely on tricks or willpower to achieve that goal. There are some spots in the world where you can't get reception, no matter how hard you try.

THE GRAND CANYON

It's one of the most popular (and breathtaking) tourist destinations in the United States—and has almost no cell phone service.

GREEN BANK, WEST VIRGINIA

Wireless signals are banned in this town, which is home to one of the world's largest radio telescopes.

GOBI DESERT, MONGOLIA

Service is so spotty here that locals are known to toss their phones in the air to catch enough of a signal to send a text.

AUSTRALIA'S RED CENTRE

In the heart of the outback, you can connect to nature—but not to Facebook.

GOING ALONE: YES OR NO?

It might seem easier to have a contemplative trip if you're on your own. But you don't need to be a wandering hermit to be mindful: there are upsides and downsides to traveling solo.

PROS:

- More time to think
- Easier to make new friends
- More self-reliant
- Complete freedom
- Forces you to speak the language
- More aware of your surroundings and other people

CONS:

- Loneliness
- Cost
- Nobody to help you solve problems
- No safety in numbers
- Nobody to create memories with
- It's easier to retreat to your devices when traveling alone

AVOID STUFFING YOUR ITINERARY

A great trip isn't about cramming in the maximum number of sites, activities, destinations, and meals. The most rewarding journeys leave plenty of blank space for wandering, reflecting, people watching, napping, and serendipity. Draft a rough schedule for your trip, choosing one or two activities to anchor each day—a meal at a certain restaurant, a hike, a museum visit—and leaving the rest up to chance and whim. An empty afternoon is a good thing, not an error that needs to be corrected.

THINK BEYOND THE HOTEL

Your attitude toward travel matters a lot more than your lodging. Still, you're more likely to have a memorable, authentic experience sleeping in a century-old farmhouse than staying in a generic chain hotel. Consider some uncommon accommodation options.

HOME RENTALS: As long as there have been travelers, there have been workaday people willing to put them up. But modern technology has made it easier than ever to rent someone else's bedroom, apartment, or house. Those homes can be cheaper than hotels—especially for families or longer stays—and often offer privacy, kitchens, and space to spread out. Even better, they give you a sense of what it's like to live in a place, not just sightsee there.

AGRITOURISM: The idea of staying in a guesthouse on a working farm started in Europe, and has been particularly popular in Italy, where these accommodations are known as *agriturismi* and number in the thousands. They're designed to allow guests to experience rural life—without having to do any farmwork—and to support agriculture. Meals made from (very) local ingredients are often part of the package. The United States has a similar concept called farm stays. Agritourism is also common in New Zealand and Australia and in other parts of Europe.

MONASTERY: You can sleep in the Vatican—and no, you don't have to join a religious order. In Europe, monasteries, like farms, offer lodging, often in historic buildings. Quarters range from spartan with shared facilities to comfortable with private baths. Some are known for their wonderful food (though others are not). Monasteries are not family-friendly, and you may be subject to rules regarding clothing, curfew—even speaking. And although these accomodations tend to be cheap, they often don't take credit cards.

CHAPTER TWO:

PREPPING AND PACKING

BUY (AND READ)
A GUIDEBOOK OR TWO

Old-fashioned paper guidebooks aren't obsolete. They have plenty of advantages over digital resources, starting with quality: the best books are based on expert research and reporting and pack all the information you might need, from the history of the destination to the best hotels and restaurants, into one portable package. They don't require a charger or an Internet connection, they can hold ticket stubs and love notes, and you can pass them on to other travelers. A guidebook might be heavier than a phone, but you can customize your own by stapling together selected sections, and you can always discard pages along the way to lighten your load.

LEARN (SOME OF) THE LANGUAGE

Becoming familiar with some of the local lingo before you go demonstrates a respect for the destination and can make it feel more familiar, give you confidence, smooth your path, and help you in a pinch. The effort is almost always appreciated and can go a long way toward fostering goodwill with your hosts—especially if they speak a more obscure tongue. These are the crucial words and phrases to learn, in order of importance.

- Hello.
- Good-bye.
- Please.
- Thank you.
- Excuse me.
- Yes and no.
- English?
- My name is _____.
- How much?
- Bathroom?
- Help!
- I'm lost.
- Cheers!

BUY A TRAVEL JOURNAL

A journal can be so much more than a record of your trip. Unlike brief and braggy Facebook posts, journaling is a way to process your experience, to express private thoughts and feelings, and to create a reference book for future travels. Remember, you don't have to write a lot, and you don't have to aim for great literature.

When choosing a journal, avoid anything too precious or expensive to throw into a bag or spill a little coffee on—no gilded pages or hand-tooled leather covers. But don't go for a cheap notebook either, as it probably won't survive the trip. Look for a hard-backed journal that's light and compact, yet large enough to allow for comfortable writing and sketching.

BECOME THE GOLDILOCKS OF PACKING

Stuff can really slow you down. Pack too much and you'll end up waiting at baggage claim and missing the train because you had to heave your big satchel up a flight of stairs. It's also a pain in the neck—and in the back, shoulders, and everywhere else. But packing too little can be a source of stress, too. Who wants to interrupt a trip to buy deodorant or a jacket?

Your goal should be to bring as much as you need and no more. Here's how to decide what to pack.

- Pack only for the things you will do, not the things you might do. The exception is a swimsuit, which often comes in handy and takes no space.
- Leave the jeans at home. They're bulky and take forever to dry.
- Think layers. Instead of a beefy sweatshirt, pack a light jacket, a vest, and a long-sleeved shirt that can be worn separately or together.
- Bring sneakers that are nice enough to wear to dinner.
- Pick a simple color palette, so everything goes together.
- Bring a big scarf (men, too). It can be repurposed as a sarong, a picnic blanket, a shawl, or even a bag.
- Invest in clothes that are designed for travel: light, versatile, and easy to wash.
- Leave the hair dryer and electric razor at home.
- Get a smaller suitcase. You'll naturally fill only as much space as you're given.
- Buy a puffy jacket that squishes down to nothing.
- Try compression bags.

MAKE HARD COPIES

Keeping all your essential information on your phone makes you dependent on having your device, a charged battery, and, often, an Internet connection. Free yourself by printing and packing these documents.

- A copy of your passport and/or driver's license and, if applicable, your visa.
- A list of emergency contacts, both local and back home.
- Phone numbers for your credit cards and banks (don't include account numbers that could be misused by a snoop or thief).
- Tickets and reservation confirmations.
- Prescriptions for important medications and for glasses and/or contacts.
- Proof of travel insurance.
- If you're leaving the country, the address and phone number of your embassy or consulate.
- Bonus points: contact information for an English-speaking doctor, clinic, or hospital in the country you're visiting.

FINISH YOUR PROJECTS

Nobody wants to ramp up his or her workload before a vacation. But tying up loose ends will make it easier to disconnect, both emotionally and electronically. Two weeks before your departure date, make a list of everything you'd like to get done, from taking out the trash to finishing a work presentation. Prioritize the "musts" and consider everything else on the list a "nice if I can." If you get to those latter tasks, that's great. If not, let yourself leave for vacation guilt-free anyway.

TAPER OFF

Although this might sound contradictory, it's a good idea to start extricating yourself from the stresses of daily life a few days before your trip begins. Consume less news. Spend less time—if any—on social media. Change your notifications so you don't get pinged every time someone shoots you an email or likes a post. Stop sleeping with your phone next to your bed. Eliminate brainless browsing time. All of this will make the transition into the mindful-travel mindset easier and faster.

CHAPTER THREE:

UNPLUGGING

WHY DIGITAL DETOXING IS GOOD FOR YOU

There are a lot of wonderful things about modern technology, and a lot of terrible ones, too. Researchers blame our phones, tablets, and other electronic devices for everything from "tech neck"—strain and bad posture from hunching over a screen—to reduced emotional intelligence. The light from screens interferes with the production of the hormone melatonin, which regulates sleep, and the high of interacting on social media can make us narcissistic and shorten our attention span. Heavy electronic use also makes us more sedentary, which means more weight gain.

The antidote is simple: pull the plug. Not much research has been devoted to the beneficial effects of digital detoxing, but anecdotal evidence suggests that people feel happier, are less anxious, and are more productive, physically active, and connected to other people when they cut back on gadget usage.

HOW DISCONNECTED DO YOU WANT TO BE?

Unplugging doesn't mean you have to abstain completely from technology. Choose a spot that works for you on the spectrum of disconnectedness. Set your goals before your trip, because if you leave your unplugging to chance or habit, you'll probably end up as absorbed in your phone as ever.

LET GO A LITTLE

If you have an unenlightened boss, need to stay in touch with family back home, or just aren't ready to go dark, you can still ratchet down your technology use. The key is to define some off-limits times, like early mornings, mealtimes, and evenings after dinner.

TAKE THE MIDDLE GROUND

Aim to go for hours—even days—without checking in. Leave your devices at your hotel when heading out for meals and sightseeing. Allow yourself scheduled check-ins, if it gives you more willpower.

CUT THE CORD COMPLETELY

It's radical but rewarding. Commit to leaving the laptop behind and keeping your phone turned off. Or don't bring a phone at all. Just leave your itinerary with someone back home in case you need to be reached.

WRITE AN EFFECTIVE OUT-OF-OFFICE (OOO) MESSAGE

Your OOO message can mean the difference between having the space to unwind and getting a call on the beach from your boss.

A successful autoreply does two things: it makes clear that people shouldn't expect to reach you, and it gives them a way to get problems solved while you're out. Keep your message brief, professional, and just detailed enough.

Here is a good example:

> I will be out of the office until June 30, and unable to reply to messages until I return. If you need assistance before then, please contact Jane Doe at janedoe12345@insertyourcompanyhere.com.

If you really want to get serious, say that you won't be reading any messages received while you're away, and that everyone will need to email you after your return date. And mean it.

Either way, consider activating your message a few hours before you leave. It takes the pressure off while you're wrapping things up, but allows you to answer the important stuff.

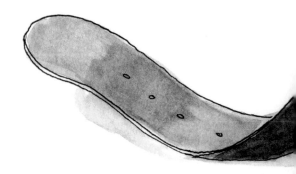

WEAR A WATCH

How often do you pick up your phone to check the time? Get yourself a real-life watch and take away the temptation (you might even make a style statement at the same time).

EMBRACE JOMO

JOMO—the Joy of Missing Out—is way better than FOMO—the Fear of Missing Out. JOMO is about letting go of being in the know, enjoying real connection instead of virtual approval, and focusing on yourself instead of everyone else (especially people you know only through their flashy Instagram feeds).

Achieving a state of JOMO may not be easy. At first, you might need to let yourself be uncomfortable—and to think about why not checking everyone else's status makes you squirm. Remember that you're probably not missing anything of actual importance, and consider the power of saying no to endless doses of affirmation or competition.

TRICK YOURSELF INTO USING LESS TECHNOLOGY

STAY ON AIRPLANE MODE

Set it before you take off, and leave it for as long as possible after you land.

LET YOUR BATTERIES DIE

Resurrect your phone only in an emergency.

PUT A TIMER ON IT

There are apps that will lock up your phone for a certain amount of time, apps that will alert you if you've been using your phone for too long, and apps that limit your access to other apps. Use them all.

FORGO THE INTERNATIONAL PLAN

The high price of connecting might make you think twice.

SCHEDULE CHECK-INS

It can be easier to unplug if you know you're going to get a guilt-free digital hit in a couple of hours. Allow yourself, say, 30 minutes online twice a day. Just make sure it's not the first thing in the morning or the last thing at night.

PLAY CELL PHONE ROULETTE

At mealtime, all the diners put their phone in the middle of the table. The first one to check his or her device foots the bill.

ASK THE HOTEL TO REMOVE THE TV

It eliminates your ability to channel surf mindlessly. If you're confident about your willpower, simply unplug it.

BUY A DUMB PHONE

They're smarter than you might think. Basic flip phones are cheap (like $20 cheap) and durable, so you don't have to freak if you lose or drop one. Because they only let you perform the simplest tasks—phone calls and texts—you have far fewer distractions.

You can find them at most big retailers, and can get them prepaid, so you don't have to sign up for a new plan. There are also minimalist mobile phones that only make and receive phone calls—the old made new again.

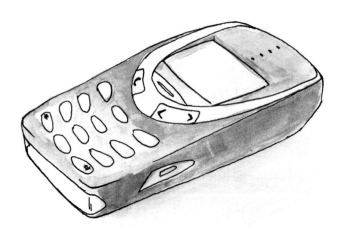

CHAPTER FOUR:
GETTING AROUND

USE A MAP, NOT AN APP

Paper maps have a lot of advantages over way-finding apps. They don't require a signal and their batteries never run out. You can mark up maps with phone numbers and favorite spots. They can be keepsakes. They can be works of art.

Sure, Google Maps can give you the fastest route. But this is traveling, not commuting. Navigating with a map slows things down. It forces you to think about context and to tune into your surroundings—street names, church spires, even the sky. Maps encourage detours and discovery. Most important, they make you—and not your phone—responsible for the journey.

HOW TO READ A MAP

- Check the orientation. North is usually at the top, though not always.
- Get a sense of the scale. Does 1 inch equal 1 mile or 10 miles?
- Figure out where you are. If you're stumped, use your position relative to two visible landmarks to triangulate your spot.
- If you're driving, watch the odometer to track how far you've traveled.
- Understand the lay of the land. When those wavy topographic lines are farther apart, the ground is flatter. When they're closer together, the ground is steeper.
- Practice. It takes a little while to stop expecting to see a little blue dot move across the map.

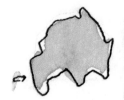

CARRY A COMPASS

If you're a hiker, you understand why this is a good idea. But a compass has more than symbolic value in a city, too. It can help you orient yourself when you can't see the sun. Coming out of a subway station in New York City confuses even locals, but a quick peek at a compass tells you which way you want to go on the grid. In a taxi, you can use it to make sure you're headed in the right general direction.

To use a compass properly, hold it as flat as you can so the needle can move freely. Turn it so the needle is lined up with the north on the dial. If you're trying to go in a certain direction, find something in the middle distance—a tall building, for instance—that corresponds to that goal, and start walking toward it.

ASK FOR DIRECTIONS

Okay, yes, it seems like a no-brainer. But it's increasingly rare to ask for directions these days, so here's your primer.

- If you can, stop in a gift shop or gas station. People who work there are used to giving directions.
- Pay attention to how confident your guide sounds. If he's hesitating and correcting himself, he may not know the area very well. Politely say thanks and then ask someone else.
- Write the directions down, if possible, as it's easy to confuse even simple instructions. Whether you record them or not, ask your guide to repeat them to be sure you heard correctly.

TAKE A RANDOM BUS ROUTE

To see parts of a city you'd otherwise miss, hop on a public bus and ride it all the way to the end of the line and back again. You may find yourself passing through neighborhoods few tourists see—ethnic enclaves, suburbs, industrial areas—and that's all part of the fun. You'll get a feel for the color and rhythm of local life. If the randomness makes you nervous, sit near the driver and embark on your excursions during daylight hours.

GET LOST—IT'S GOOD FOR YOU

In normal life, being lost is a bad thing. But when you're traveling, it can yield all kinds of wonderful results. You might discover a neighborhood, a park, or a hilltop view that you never would have experienced otherwise. Being lost instantly makes you more attentive and aware of your surroundings. It may make you feel vulnerable, too, but that won't harm you. Allowing yourself to be lost teaches you to go with the flow. And getting your bearings back requires putting your problem-solving skills to use.

TAKE PUBLIC TRANSPORTATION

Depending on where you're traveling, using local transit can be either a crowded, confusing trip or an exercise in cleanliness and efficiency. No matter: get on that trolley, subway, bus, or ferry. Public transportation is how the locals get around, and going with them immerses you in the culture (and makes for good people watching). It's cheap, environmentally friendly, and contributes to keeping such systems running. And because you need to figure out your way from point A to point B, it makes you an active participant in the journey, not just a passenger.

CHAPTER FIVE:

CONNECTING WITH PEOPLE

LEARN HOW TO SAY HELLO

A handshake isn't a kiss isn't a bow isn't a nose rub. Learning the local greeting customs shows respect for others and can spare you some awkward situations.

- In Japan, it's common for men and women to bow when encountering someone.
- In northern Europe, a handshake is the norm between strangers.
- In Thailand, the *wai*—pressing your hands together prayer-like in front of your heart and bowing slightly—is traditional.
- In India, it's rude to touch someone of the opposite sex.
- In France, kisses on alternate cheeks is customary for both sexes, even when meeting someone for the first time.

START A CONVERSATION

It's an art worth learning.

First, break the ice, without making it seem forced or artificial. Start with a simple request: Can you take my photo? Is someone sitting here? Do you have the time? Or compliment the person on something he or she is wearing or carrying.

If you get friendly vibes in return, follow up with something appropriate: What's a great place to eat around here? Where did you get those sneakers? Are you from here? Don't engage in vague queries. Asking a random stranger certain questions—how are you? how's it going?—would be uncomfortable for both of you.

Have a few fallbacks for avoiding unnerving questions or getting out of awkward conversations: I don't know—what do you think? It's a complicated issue, isn't it? Thanks for the chat, but I've got to go!

LISTEN LIKE YOU MEAN IT

Listening is a skill that translates around the world. According to experts, a good listener has the following habits.

- Focuses on the speaker
- Practices silence
- Avoids interrupting
- Makes eye contact
- Asks questions
- Doesn't worry about what to say next

SPREAD THE CHEERS

Every country and culture has a different way to toast. Knowing how to do it in the local style will endear you to hosts—and to strangers at the bar. No matter where you are in the world, try to keep it casual, confident, and friendly.

- In Denmark, the host or older person traditionally toasts first. Sip after the host and say *skål* (SKOAL).
- In France, say *santé* (sahn-TAY) and clink glasses while looking into the other person's eyes. When toasting around the table, be sure not to cross arms.
- In China, the host makes the first toast, saying *ganbei* (gon-bay) and raising a glass. For that first one, clink the bellies of your glasses. Guests toast for the rest of the night, and if the group is large, you can just tap your glass on the table, rather than clink.
- In Israel, raise your drink and say *l'chaim* (luh HY-im), which means "to life."

BECOME A REGULAR

If you find a coffee shop, food truck, bookstore, or restaurant you like, don't make it a one-time visit. Go back a second time, and a third. Say hi. After a couple of days, the staff will start to recognize you. In a small way, you will become part of the community and feel more connected to the place you're visiting. The employees may start treating you like a friend, offering chitchat, guidance, and even invitations.

WORSHIP WITH THE LOCALS

It's one thing to visit a church or a temple to admire the architecture. To better understand local life, attend an actual service. Seek permission beforehand, if possible, since policies vary from religion to religion and country to country. (In some regions, non-Muslims aren't welcome in mosques, for instance, but in others they are.) Needless to say, be quiet and respectful. Dress appropriately—in many religions that means covering your arms, legs, and sometimes your head. (Bring a scarf as a precaution and wear socks in case you're asked to remove your shoes.) Enjoy the beauty of the ritual. And if anyone asks, you don't have to feel awkward. Just say that you are visiting and would like to learn.

CHAPTER SIX:

IMMERSING YOURSELF

DON'T FIGHT JET LAG

Everyone seems to have a secret remedy for jet lag: sunglasses, swimming, pills, changing sleep patterns in the days before the flight. But maybe jet lag isn't something you should be trying to correct.

It's natural for your body to want to maintain its normal schedule. What's not natural is speeding around the globe in an oversize tin can. So go with your instincts and sleep when you're tired, even if that's in the middle of the morning, and don't force yourself to slumber. Live sans schedule for a little while and you just might be rewarded with rich and surprising experiences— the sounds of a city coming to life before dawn, the sight of a sunrise over the sea, the joys of reading a book in the dead of night.

SET YOUR DAILY INTENTIONS

It's similar to determining your intentions for your trip (see page 8), but on a smaller scale. Do you want this to be a physical day or a quiet, meditative one? Do you want to be adventurous or play it safe? Don't turn this into a big, time-consuming decision. Think about it while you're brushing your teeth or having breakfast, then once you've made your choice, go out and do it.

TAKE UP A HANDS-ON HOBBY

Be a maker, not a swiper. Hobbies like knitting, whittling, sketching (see page 65), and crocheting give your hands something to reach for instead of a phone.

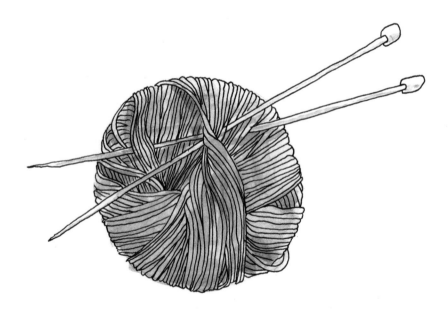

BRING A BOOK—IT'S BETTER THAN A KINDLE

Reading a book on a tablet is not always the best thing. Sure, e-readers are light and convenient and let you read almost any book you want instantly. But studies have shown that people absorb less of what they read on a screen and that devices can mess with your sleep.

Consider all the advantages real books offer. You can leave them lying around without worrying that they'll be stolen. Books won't get broken in your bag or at the beach. They don't need to be plugged in. They can be repositories for notes. Instead of expensive gadgets that can create a gap between you and people who have less, they can be conversation starters— and be left behind as gifts.

REVIVE THE LOST ART OF POSTCARD WRITING

Mailing postcards to friends and family back home used to be a travel ritual. But postcards aren't dead—and it's more of a delight than ever to receive one. Here is your writing refresher.

- Include the date.
- Skip the questions (no one is writing you back).
- Sign it clearly so your identity isn't a mystery.
- Try to distill your trip into a few sentences.
- Write down a fun fact (or five).
- Make it personal. Did something you saw, ate, or heard make you think of the person to whom you're writing?
- When you buy a postcard, ask if the shop sells stamps—and if not, where they're sold nearby.

KEEP A SKETCH JOURNAL

Even if you don't consider yourself an artist, capturing a place in drawings can be magical. It's a different way of thinking and engaging with your surroundings. Don't get intimidated: this is about the process, not the results. Also, you don't have to show it to anyone. Ever.

If you're stumped for a starting point, try focusing on a single subject, such as a cup of coffee, a roof, or a face. Make sketching a regular habit, and if it helps, give yourself a time limit. To heighten your interest, try different techniques, such as completing an entire drawing with a single line, drawing upside down, or sketching a cartoon or caricature.

Pocket-size sketch books are available, though any notebook will do. There are even books with pages that can be torn out for postcards, if you end up especially pleased with your work. Almost nothing is as special as receiving a hand-drawn missive from far away.

PEOPLE WATCH WISELY

Observing other people is one of life's great pleasures, whether you're close to home or far away. It's fun to play amateur anthropologist, making observations about human behavior and culture, and filling in backstories with your imagination.

The location can make or break your people-watching experience. Look for a spot that's unobtrusive but offers a good view. A seat at a place where people are going in and out—a train station, a café, a park—can be great. Be respectful of others, even though they are in public. Don't stare or be creepy. (Wearing sunglasses can let you get away with more direct looking.)

Don't know how to start? You might seek out lookalikes—people who resemble celebrities or friends back home. Or see what inferences you can make about people just by observing them. Who are they? What do they do for a living? Where are they going? What mood are they in? What are you learning from the people about this place, including habits, manners, and culture? Can you discern any subcultures?

LOOK AT CONTEMPORARY ART

Contemporary art—work by living artists, or made after World War II—can be beautiful, arresting, and awe inspiring. It can also be challenging, confusing, or uncomfortable. And it's worth seeking out. Just as art from the past is a window into the culture, society, and politics of a certain era, contemporary art is a way to see the modern world through the eyes of the most creative people.

There are no rules when it comes to viewing art (except, in most cases, don't touch). But to engage fully, come with an open mind. Don't immediately judge anything you see as bad or nonsensical. Once you consider it, you may decide it doesn't speak to you or it isn't good art. Always accept it for what it is, however, not what you think art should be. Consider how it was created, what it might have meant to the artist, and what it says about when and where it was made.

You may not find contemporary art in local museums. It might instead be in galleries, or even on the street. If you're staying in a hotel, ask the concierge for advice on where to find it.

GET FAMILIAR WITH THE FLORA AND FAUNA

"To name is to pay attention; to name is to love," observes writer Maria Popova. There's a deep sense of connection that comes when you can identify the birds, flowers, and trees that populate a place. The foreign becomes familiar, the general becomes particular. It's an intimate way to know a destination.

You don't have to be on a safari or conservation trip to get to know the local wildlife. And you don't have to be in a destination known for its exotica— though it's certainly easier to find books about the wildlife of Costa Rica and Botswana than, say, Portugal. Try the back pages of your guidebook or buy a specialty guide. The Travellers' Wildlife Guides series covers several countries, and The Sibley Guides series is a must for birders. If you want to stay plugged in, there are also apps devoted to identifying plants and animals.

GIVE YOURSELF PERMISSION TO BE LAZY

It can be very tempting to go, go, go—to try to maximize your vacation time by piling up the activities and hustling from one thing to the next. But often, less really is more. Perpetual busyness strains our nervous and immune systems. It keeps us from relaxing and enjoying our surroundings.

On your next trip, go where your whims direct you. When you're feeling tired, stop. When you're enjoying a place, stay there. The rewards will be an increased sense of relaxation, a greater ability to be present, and heightened creativity and reflection.

SCHEDULE NAPS

A siesta is one of the simplest and most powerful indulgences. Naps boost imagination and alertness, reduce stress, and improve health. Build naps into your daily travel schedule to help your mind process all the new experiences—and even languages—of a trip, and just because naps make you feel good.

WATCH THE SUNRISE OR SUNSET

No matter how many times you've watched the sun emerge from or disappear below the horizon, the experience never gets old. It's probably beautiful no matter where you are. And in some places, it just might be the highlight of a trip, a moment to reflect on bigness and smallness, to revel in heavenly color, and to feel connected to nature and the cosmos.

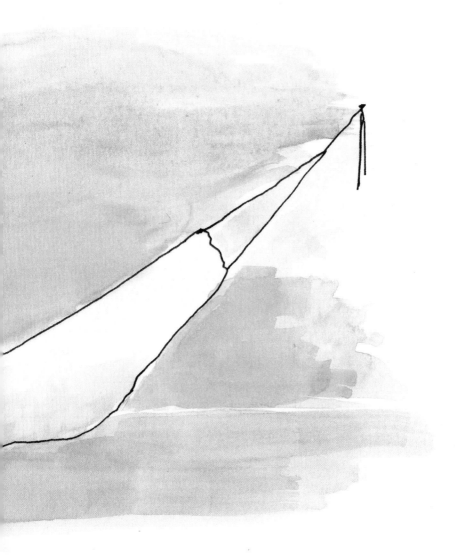

TAKE OFF YOUR SHOES

Call it "earthing" if you want to get fancy. The rest of us like to call it "going barefoot." It's said to boost your immune system and improve your blood health. But you can do it just for the pleasure of feeling grass, sand, or mud on your feet. (Just keep your shoes on when traveling in any place where there might be animal droppings, which can spread nasty parasites.)

FIND SOME QUIET SPACE

It's easy to get overwhelmed in urban areas. But even in the biggest, busiest cities, it's possible to find pockets of peace. Try botanical gardens, college campuses, smaller museums, libraries, and places of worship. In airports, look for the chapel—or just an empty gate.

MEMORIZE A MOMENT

Each day, choose a moment to commit to your memory bank. Pay attention to every detail—sights, sounds, smells. Consider the temperature and the quality of the light. Note how you feel. Observe the colors of umbrellas, signs, carpets, leaves. Roll the scene over in your mind and describe it to yourself with your eyes closed. Write a diary entry in your head.

CHAPTER SEVEN:
EATING AND DRINKING

FIND THE BEST MEAL, ANYWHERE IN THE WORLD

Skip Yelp, forget Foursquare, and don't bother with the hotel concierge. This is how to find the greatest spots to dig in.

TALK TO TAXI DRIVERS

They know the city inside and out.

KNOW HOW TO ASK

Don't ask, where should I eat? Instead ask, where do *you* like to eat? It might sound like a subtle difference, but it's more likely to yield local favorites, rather than tourist spots.

FOLLOW THE CROWDS

If that hole in the wall has a line of locals going out the door, get in it.

EXPLORE ETHNIC NEIGHBORHOODS

You'll almost certainly find authentic, affordable, delectable fare.

GRILL THE STAFF

Once you find a killer restaurant, ask the server, chef, host, and busser to recommend other great places. They're probably bigger foodies than you are and will know exactly what's worth visiting.

TAKE A FOOD TOUR

These tours tend to be geared toward (and run by) gourmands and typically spotlight lesser-known establishments. Or consider signing up for a home-cooked meal. A number of start-ups, including Traveling Spoon, CookApp, Feastly, and EatWith, are there to help.

MIND YOUR PLATE

Have you gotten so used to eating at your desk that you've forgotten what it's like to savor a meal? Use these techniques to be present at the table.

EAT WITH THE WRONG HAND

Because it's more difficult, it forces you to pay attention to each mouthful. This may be a little much for every meal, but try it once in a while as a resetting tool.

PUT YOUR FORK DOWN BETWEEN BITES

It automatically slows down the meal and encourages you to chew thoroughly, think about your food, and look around.

PLAY "NAME THE INGREDIENTS"

Make your meal into a guessing game. Focus on the texture, flavors, and aromas in your food and try to identify as many components as possible. Is that almond? Could that be seaweed? Do I detect cardamom?

EMBARK ON A FOOD QUEST

Pick a cuisine or dish you love or want to explore—anything from Indian food to New England lobster rolls. Build your trip (or even a day) around finding the best or most interesting versions of your choice. That narrows your food focus and gets you thinking deeply about one thing. It turns a trip into a treasure hunt. Wherever you eat, make sure to ask questions: How do you make it? What's your secret or your secret ingredient? What else should I try?

LEARN TO EAT ALONE

It can be one of the most intimidating dining experiences, even when you're in a familiar place. But it can also be highly rewarding—peaceful, meditative, liberating, even life-changing.

Start with breakfast, if you like, since you probably won't be the only person eating solo. You can bring a book, newspaper, or notebook, but leave your phone behind.

If you're open to talking to other people, sit at the bar. Enjoy watching other diners and imagining their backstories. Feel free to eavesdrop. Focus on your food—the flavors, textures, smells, how it's arranged on the plate. Food writer Simran Sethi says that dining alone at a restaurant made her realize the interdependence involved in every meal. So as you eat, reflect on the fact that you are not actually alone: your meal connects you to a whole bunch of people, from farmers, harvesters, buyers, truckers, and fishermen to butchers, bakers, servers, chefs, bussers, and more. Oh, and order whatever you like, even if it's three desserts. There's nobody across the table to judge you!

TRY A NEW FOOD EVERY DAY

That goes double if you're an unadventurous eater. You don't have to start (or end) with fish eyes (unless you are in southern China, where they are prized). But new tastes expand your palate and also make you think about what you normally eat and don't eat, and why. Bonus points for working your way up to something crazy.

TAKE A COOKING LESSON

Learning how to cook is a way to immerse yourself in the local cuisine as well as connect with other food lovers—especially in places where food is a preoccupation, like Italy, Thailand, Japan, or Mexico.

CHAPTER EIGHT:
PICTURE-PERFECT TRAVEL

RECALL THE JOYS OF 35MM FILM

Taking photos with film is slow. It offers only two or three dozen shots per roll. You might have to wait several days to see the results. And that's exactly why it's so wonderful.

There's romance and ritual to using film—flicking open the camera to load a new roll, setting the tab on its spool, winding the film back up at the end, clutching a mysterious cache of images in your fist. It's the opposite of instant gratification: only when you see the prints will you know what you shot. When you're taking a photograph, you shoot less and think more. And when you're done, you don't just have a chip packed with bits and bytes, but a memory made tangible, framable, and findable years later in a desk drawer.

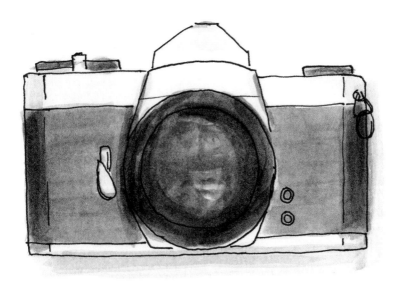

CONSIDER LEAVING THE CAMERA AT HOME

You think you're capturing memories with photos, but in many cases, the only place they will live is on a hard drive. Research has shown that taking a photograph of an experience makes you less likely to remember it. Leaving the camera behind puts you back in the present, seeing the world through your eyes (#nofilter) instead of through a lens or a digital screen. It also keeps you from being an obnoxious, selfie stick–wielding tourist.

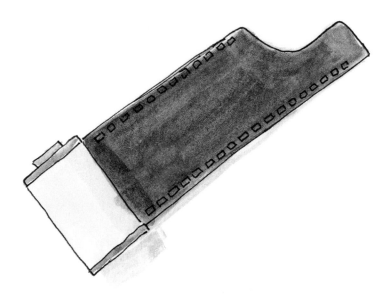

TAKE ONLY A FEW PHOTOS EACH DAY

Whether you're shooting with your phone or on film, limiting the number of photographs you take forces you to put quality over quantity. You'll look more closely and think more deeply about your surroundings. You'll skip the forgettable stuff, the generic every-tourist shot. You'll think about what's powerful and important. And you'll spend less time fumbling with a screen, adding filters, and obsessing about the minute differences among photographs. To further force yourself to take fewer pictures, install a smaller memory card in your digital camera.

PHOTOGRAPH A FEELING

Instead of just shooting what looks pretty or interesting, bring more depth to your pictures by giving yourself the task of capturing an emotion. You can decide on a feeling—joy, frustration, exhaustion, contentment—and then look for a shot with that feeling and try to frame it in your photograph. Or you can simply look for any strong emotion and capture that. This exercise gets you beneath the surface and pushes you to tune into your surroundings in a different way.

THINK LIKE A PHOTOJOURNALIST

Go beyond attractiveness and try to tell a story with your picture. Attempt to capture a relationship, a contrast, or a challenge, or try to provoke a question—or questions. Who are those people? What are they doing? Why are they doing it? Taking photos like that requires your full attention and for all your senses to be open. Don't be afraid to get up close, to shoot action, or to consider themes, like symmetry, decay, or affection.

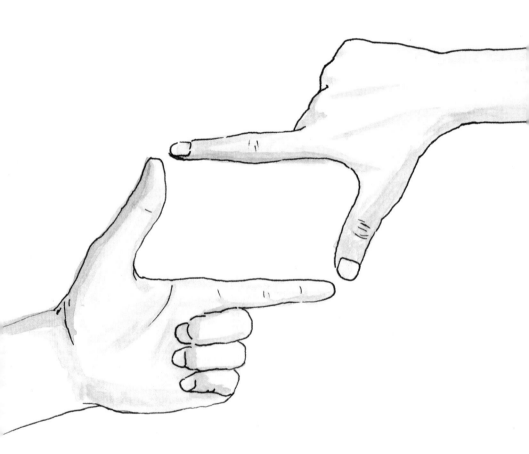

CHAPTER NINE:

WHEN THINGS GO WRONG

EXPECT COMPLICATIONS

It's the rare trip that goes completely pear-shaped, but on almost every journey something will go, well, differently than you expected. You're on the move in unfamiliar places, dependent on lots of systems and people to perform just right. There will be delayed flights, missed trains, lost reservations, bad hotel rooms. You might get sick. You might get hurt. If you expect your trip to be "perfect," you're almost certain to be let down. But if you accept that it will be perfectly real, you're sure to be satisfied.

FIGURE OUT HOW TO COPE

Psychologists describe two stress-reducing ways to deal with mishaps. Problem-focused coping is about fixing what can be changed. It is not about trying to figure out why it happened, and it is definitely not about wallowing in self-pity. Missed your flight? Start calling airline reps.

Emotion-focused coping is trying to feel better about what happened because you can't fix or change it. Missed your flight? Get an ice cream. Enjoy the extra day in your destination. Consider how freeing it can be to stay in the limbo of an airport hotel.

MEDITATE (OR DO YOGA) ON THE GO

No mat, no studio, no teacher? No problem. You can still use relaxation, focusing, and stretching techniques on the road. And they can be especially powerful when your journey goes awry.

The first step is to breathe. Although it sounds obvious, it too often isn't in a moment of crisis. Take one minute—literally—to close your eyes and pay attention to your breath going in and out. Don't try to change it; just observe it. If you're having trouble focusing, count your breaths and see how high you can go.

Another on-the-go meditation approach is to tune into a sound. Close your eyes and turn your full attention to the rumble of the engine, the bustle of the crowd, or the rattle of a train car rolling along the tracks. Just listen as wholly as you can.

Make up a mantra. It might be as simple as, "Everything will be okay." Repeating it distractedly won't do much good. Concentrate on it. Breathe it in and out. Let it suffuse your body and mind.

If you've ever dipped a toe in yoga, you know several poses and progressions that can be done without a mat. A standing forward bend, where you reach your head toward the floor; a tree pose, in which you balance on one leg while the other foot is tucked against your thigh; and a standing back bend are just three possibilities.

KNOW THAT BAD EXPERIENCES MAKE THE BEST STORIES

Everyone wants to hear about your luxurious, pleasant, not-a-ripple trip—for about five seconds. It's the tales of debacle and disaster, of being lost and screwing up, of "there was this one time when . . ." that have staying power and can provide entertainment and lessons for years to come.

REMEMBER WHAT YOUR MOTHER SAID

No, seriously, what's the worst that can happen? Unless you are in a life-threatening situation, the worst is generally not that terrible. You might miss some of your vacation. You can replace that lost phone, camera, passport, whatever. You won't miss that $100 in a year. So let it go.

KNOW WHOM TO CALL

Luggage gets lost. Illnesses and injuries happen. When bad things occur on a trip, it helps to know whom to contact for help.

- If your luggage gets lost: Don't leave the airport. Report it to the airline and don't exit the building until an airline representative supplies you with a written report of your loss, as well as details (in writing) on what you can purchase to replace your belongings.
- If you lose your passport: Go straight to your nearest embassy or consulate. Hopefully you have a photocopy of your passport with you (see page 24), which will help speed the process along.
- If you get sick: Go to a drugstore. In many countries, pharmacists can diagnose minor illnesses and dispense medication. If you're seriously ill, call the US embassy or consulate and ask for a list of local English-speaking doctors.
- If you get hurt: Go to the nearest big-city hospital. A taxi driver will usually know where it is.

CHAPTER TEN:

TRAVELING WITH KIDS

LET THE KIDS HELP PLAN THE TRIP

Getting your children involved in the planning gets them involved in the trip. Just as they're more likely to eat something they helped cook, they're more likely to enjoy an escape they helped organize. Giving kids a role cuts down on complaining later (or at least gives you a good comeback). It's a chance for them to learn about money, research, geography, and transportation—and an opportunity for you to learn about your kids.

IS IT POSSIBLE TO DO A MINDFUL TRIP WITH KIDS?

In some ways, it's harder to be a present traveler with children in tow. You have less quiet time and alone time, and being in charge of small people can be stressful, as they introduce logistical complications (like car seats and diaper changes).

But in other ways, it's easier. Kids tend to be more present than adults. So much is new to them, and they marvel at sights that many adults would barely take note of, like a small pile of rocks at the beach, a doorstop in the shape of a cow, or the funny lady at the museum shop. They also ask surprisingly thoughtful questions, like "Where do the rainbows go?"

Traveling as a family is an exercise in flexibility and going with the flow, not to mention being a role model for patience and consideration. Teaching children, seeing the world through their eyes, and simply being by their side through new experiences can bring you closer to one another—and to being more present in the world.

SET EXPECTATIONS IN ADVANCE

Don't just tell your children that you're going to Florida. Especially if they're younger or haven't traveled much, it's important to talk to kids about how you'll get there, what you'll be doing once you're there, what you might see, and what behavior is expected. What they can and cannot do on an airplane or in a hotel won't be obvious to them.

Discussing the trip ahead of time both builds excitement and allays fears. And it's easier to remind children that they're not supposed to kick the seat in front of them than to explain for the first time why it's a problem.

PUT LIMITS ON DEVICES

There's a time and a place for gadgets. They can help get kids through long flights, for example. And as the kids get older, it can get harder to take them away. But regardless of your child's age, it's wise to set some rules in advance about screen time. Establish the same kinds of boundaries with kids as you set for yourself, such as no electronic devices at meals or at the beach. Agree to put everyone's phone in a safe or the glove compartment to reduce temptation.

SET OFF ALONE

It's not about taking a break from your traveling companions. (Okay, it is a little bit.) But getting a coffee on your own or spending a morning exploring solo gives your trip contrast. Knowing that you'll be worrying about only yourself for a while, you'll suddenly feel light and swift. You'll have more mental space for observation and immersion, and you'll get a reminder of what it's like to blend in.

TEACH THEM HOW TO NAVIGATE

For smaller kids, this might be as simple as introducing the concepts of north, south, east, and west, then letting them use your compass (see page 42) and showing them the basics of maps. Teach older children about map legends, contour lines, and highway exit numbers. Give them a map and your destination and let them figure out how to navigate from A to B. Play being lost and ask them how they would begin to find their way back to the hotel, looking for landmarks and other cues.

BRING BACK ROAD-TRIP GAMES

You remember them . . . or do you? Here's a refresher on classic diversions, no batteries required.

I'M GOING ON A PICNIC

It starts with one person saying, "I'm going on a picnic, and I'm taking . . ." then choosing an item that starts with A. The next person repeats the whole sentence, adds a B item, and so on through the alphabet. To make the game more difficult, add rules, such as everything taken to the picnic must be red.

20 QUESTIONS

One person thinks of something and announces the category, such as a person/place/thing or animal/vegetable/mineral. The other player or players then have 20 yes/no questions to figure out what it is.

I SPY

Great for small kids. The first player chooses an object that's within sight and says, "I spy with my little eye . . ." and adds a hint, such as "something that is blue," or "something that starts with C." The other player or players try to guess what it is, and the one who guesses right takes the next turn as spy.

THE NAME GAME

One person starts by saying the name of someone famous. The next person has to name a famous person whose first name starts with the same letter as the last name of the previous round, and so on until everyone is stuck.

RADIO ROULETTE

It's not exactly a game, but it will keep you thinking. Set an interval, like every 10 minutes, to change to a random radio station. You might end up listening to folk music, rap, opera, jazz, political talk, or religious radio.

CHAPTER ELEVEN:

COMING HOME

MAKE A VACATION RESOLUTION

Before your trip ends, decide on a change that you will bring back to your usual routine. It might be a daily meditation or yoga practice. Or maybe it's a local custom that you'd like to integrate into life back home, like sundowners or afternoon tea. Commit now or it will likely slip away.

RETURN ON A THURSDAY

If you work regular office hours, coming home midweek means you have only one or two days in the office before the weekend. It's a way to dip back into regular worklife and then spend Saturday and Sunday acclimatising and catching up before working a full work week.

STAY IN TOUCH

Don't let all the email addresses of the many great people you met while traveling languish. In a few weeks the memories will have faded, and you'll wonder if there's any point in reaching out. So do it now, while the connection is still fresh. Friend them on social media. Drop them a note saying it was nice to meet them and recounting something pleasant that happened. Start planning a reunion.

TACK ON A STAYCATION DAY

It's tempting to squeeze as much travel as you can out of your vacation days. But a day off after you return lets you transition back home with less stress. You can unpack, restock the fridge, go to a movie, eke out one more afternoon nap. That extra day is especially helpful if you'll be jet-lagged.

DON'T BE A HERO

It can be easy to sink into a work panic after a trip, especially an extended vacation. That's a recipe for stress and unhappiness and will undo all the unwinding you did while away. Try to ease into regular life when you return.

- Leave your out-of-office message on for an extra day.
- Go out for dinner or cook a lovely meal.
- Leave the office at the normal time, if possible.
- Take it slow on digital reintegration. Reintroduce apps one at a time—or try not to use them at all.
- Avoid overscheduling yourself in your first few days back home.
- Build in some reflection or meditation time.
- Try to think about the big picture. What do you really want or need to accomplish in the next week? What's important?

CONFRONT THE EMAIL BEAST

If you followed the advice on page 32 and told everyone that messages that arrived while you were away would be ignored, you have only one (bold) step to take when you return to work: delete them.

The rest of you have a mountain of messages to process. To keep from feeling overwhelmed, have a strategy for tackling it. You might scroll through the list and flag the most important emails, then answer them first. You could take the opposite approach and quickly delete everything unimportant to reduce the volume. Or decide that you will process only 10 emails at a time, take a break, then do 10 more. Just make sure to pick a plan and stick to it.

REFLECT ON YOUR JOURNEY

Too often we return from vacation and immediately immerse ourselves in everyday life. Weeks later, when we dump our photos online, we give the trip a passing thought. This time, set aside some space to think about the experience you just had and what it meant to you. Review your journal. Browse through your photos and choose a couple to print or share. Before you fall asleep, roll the memories around in your mind so they will stay with you.

ACKNOWLEDGMENTS

I wouldn't have written this book without Nick Fauchald, who had the fantastic idea in the first place, and Jessica Flint, who generously connected us. Endless thanks to my grandmother and my mother, brave travelers in the world and in life; Drew, my husband and soulmate; and Jack and Lia. I love you more than the moon and the stars.

ABOUT THE AUTHOR

Sara Clemence took her first international trip at the age of nine, when instead of starting fifth grade, she spent three months traveling around China with her family. She has been a travel editor at *The Wall Street Journal* and *Travel + Leisure*. Her writing has appeared in those publications, as well as in *Vogue*, *Esquire*, *Forbes*, *Marie Claire*, *Redbook*, and many others. She lives in New York with her husband and two children, and finally has a passport photo she likes.

PIATKUS

First published in the US in 2017 by Dovetail Press in Brooklyn, New York, a division of Assembly Brands LLC.

First published in Great Britain in 2018 by Piatkus

1 3 5 7 9 10 8 6 4 2

Text copyright © Sara Clemence 2018
Design and Illustrations by Chris Santone

The moral right of the author has been asserted.

All rights reserved.

No part of this publication may be reproduced, stored in a retrieval system, or transmitted in any form or by any means, without the prior permission in writing of the publisher, nor be otherwise circulated in any form of binding or cover other than that in which it is published and without a similar condition including this condition being imposed on the subsequent purchaser.

A CIP catalogue record for this book is available from the British Library.

ISBN 978-0-349-42162-9

Printed and bound in Italy by L.E.G.O SpA

Papers used by Piatkus are from well-managed forests and other responsible sources.

Piatkus
An imprint of
Little, Brown Book Group
Carmelite House
50 Victoria Embankment
London EC4Y 0DZ

An Hachette UK Company
www.hachette.co.uk

www.improvementzone.co.uk